USBORNE FIRST NATURE

CREEPY CRAWLIES

CATHY KILPATRICK

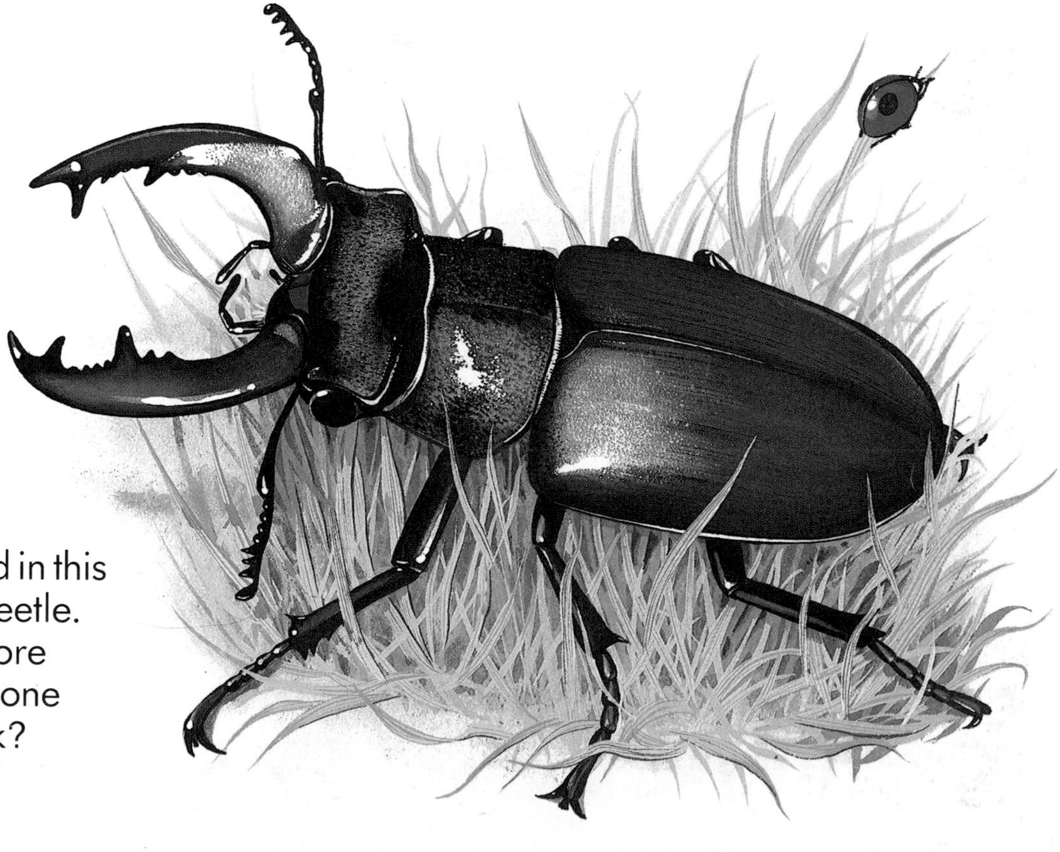

There is a Ladybird in this picture of a Stag Beetle. Can you find 10 more Ladybirds like this one hidden in this book?

Looking at insects and other small animals

This book is about animals called invertebrates, which means "no backbone". They have no skeleton inside their body. Most of the different kinds of invertebrates are insects, but not all. On these pages you can see the six groups of land invertebrates described in this book.

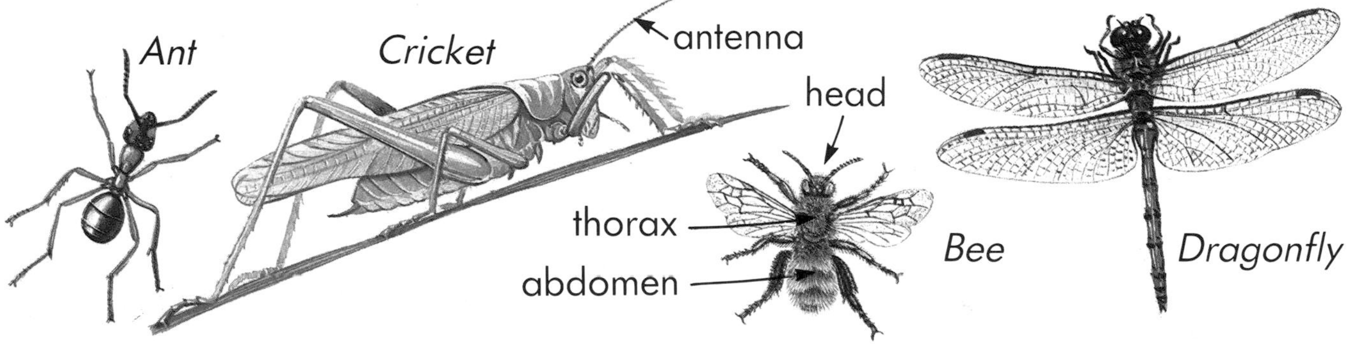

These are just four of the thousands of different kinds of insects. All adult insects have six legs and three parts to their body. They have a head, a middle section called the thorax, and an end section called the abdomen. On the head are two feelers called antennae. Most insects have wings at some stage in their lives.

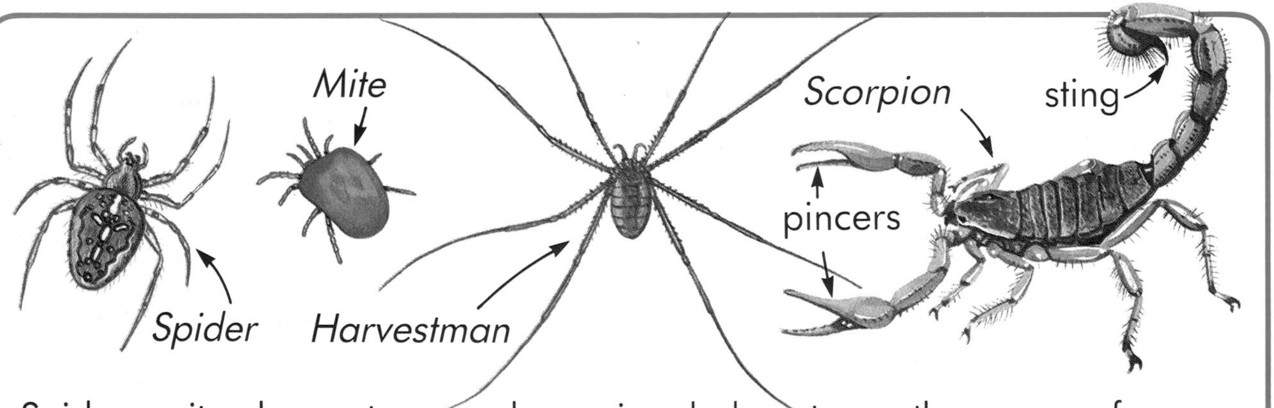

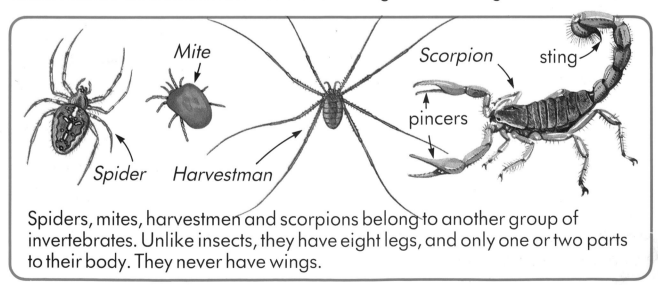

Spiders, mites, harvestmen and scorpions belong to another group of invertebrates. Unlike insects, they have eight legs, and only one or two parts to their body. They never have wings.

Millipedes and centipedes have the most legs of any invertebrate.

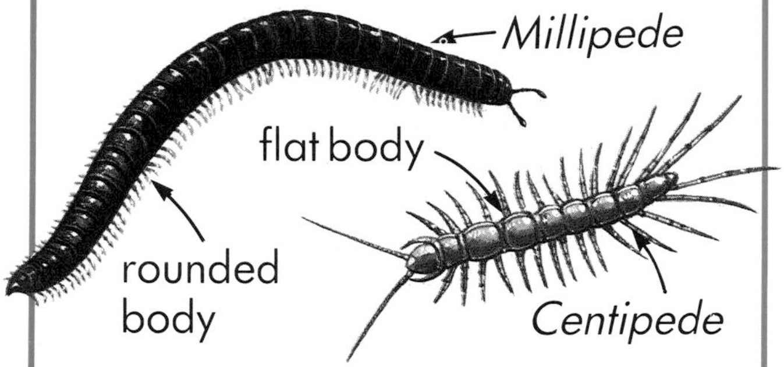

Their body is divided into a head and many rings, called segments. Most centipedes have 30 legs, while some millipedes have up to 700. They both have feelers.

Woodlice usually have a flat body divided into several segments.

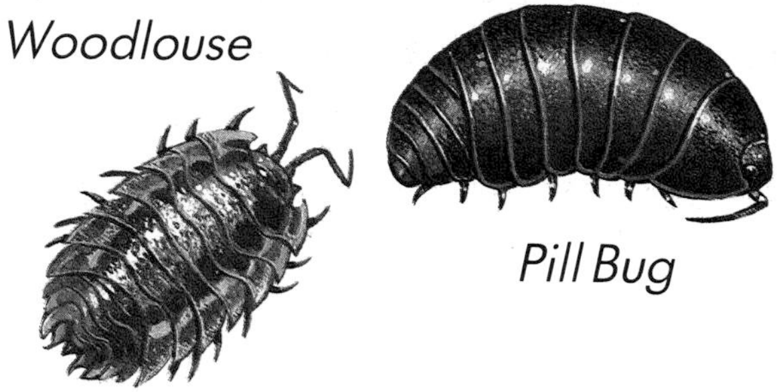

They have 14 legs that are used for walking and 2 that are used for feeding. Woodlice are also called sow-bugs and slaters. Pill Bugs are woodlice that can roll into a ball.

Worms, like millipedes and centipedes, have many segments in their body.

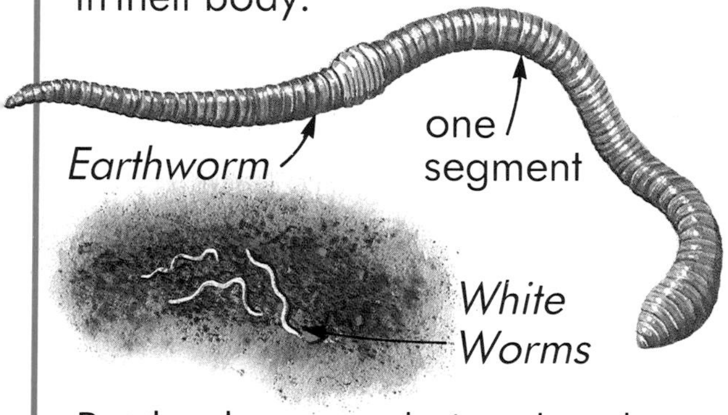

But they have no obvious head, no feelers, and they never have legs. However, they do have a mouth opening at the front end.

Slugs and snails belong to yet another group of invertebrates.

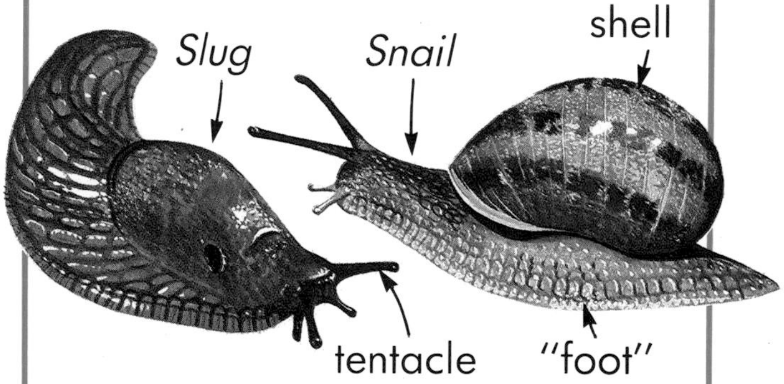

They both move on a muscular "foot" and have one or two pairs of tentacles. Snails have a shell on their backs but slugs do not.

How invertebrates move

Many insects can fly, using one or two pairs of wings. Some can fly very fast – a Dragonfly can do 40 kilometres an hour.

A beetle has two pairs of wings.

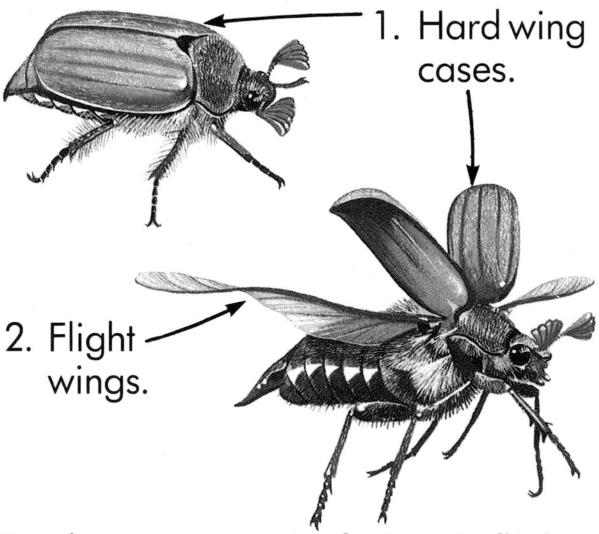

Beetles use one pair of wings in flight. They hold the wing cases out and move the flight wings up and down.

Bees use two pairs of wings in flight but it looks like one pair. Special hooks join the pairs of wings together.

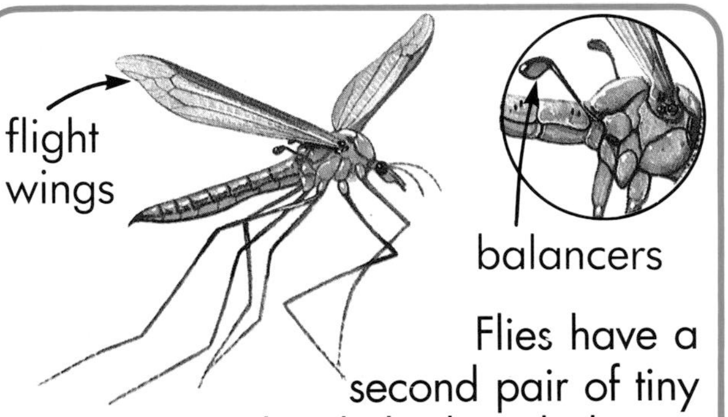

Flies have a second pair of tiny wings instead to help them balance.

How the wings move in flight

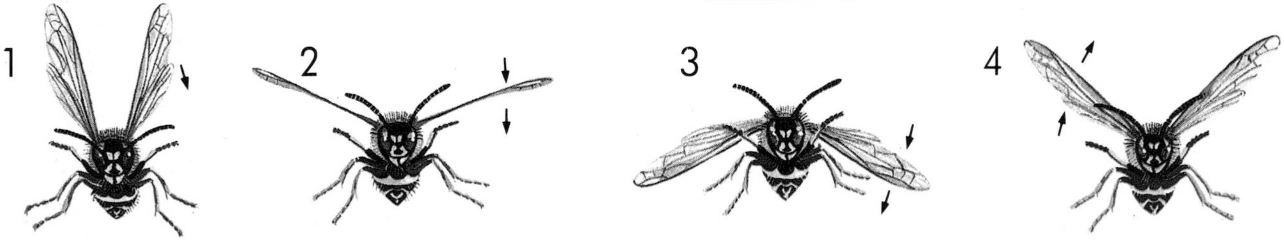

During the down stroke, the wings push the air downwards and backwards.

The up stroke of the wings.

Walking, jumping and crawling

This is a looper caterpillar. It brings its back legs up to the front legs and then moves the front legs forwards.

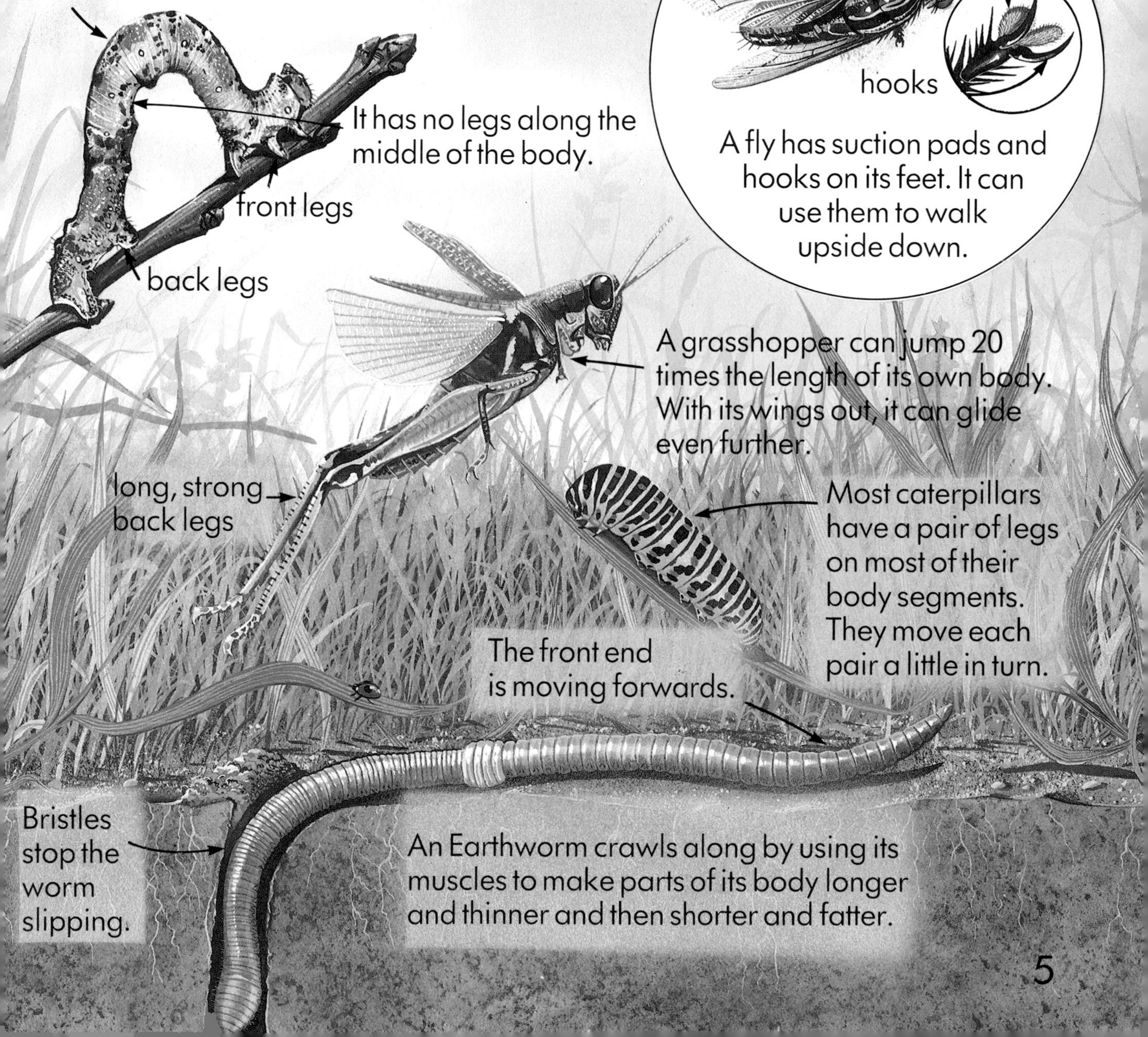

It has no legs along the middle of the body.

A fly has suction pads and hooks on its feet. It can use them to walk upside down.

A grasshopper can jump 20 times the length of its own body. With its wings out, it can glide even further.

Most caterpillars have a pair of legs on most of their body segments. They move each pair a little in turn.

An Earthworm crawls along by using its muscles to make parts of its body longer and thinner and then shorter and fatter.

How invertebrates feed

There are thousands of different invertebrates. They do not all find food or eat in the same way. Some eat plants, others eat animals or both animals and plants. A few invertebrates feed on blood.

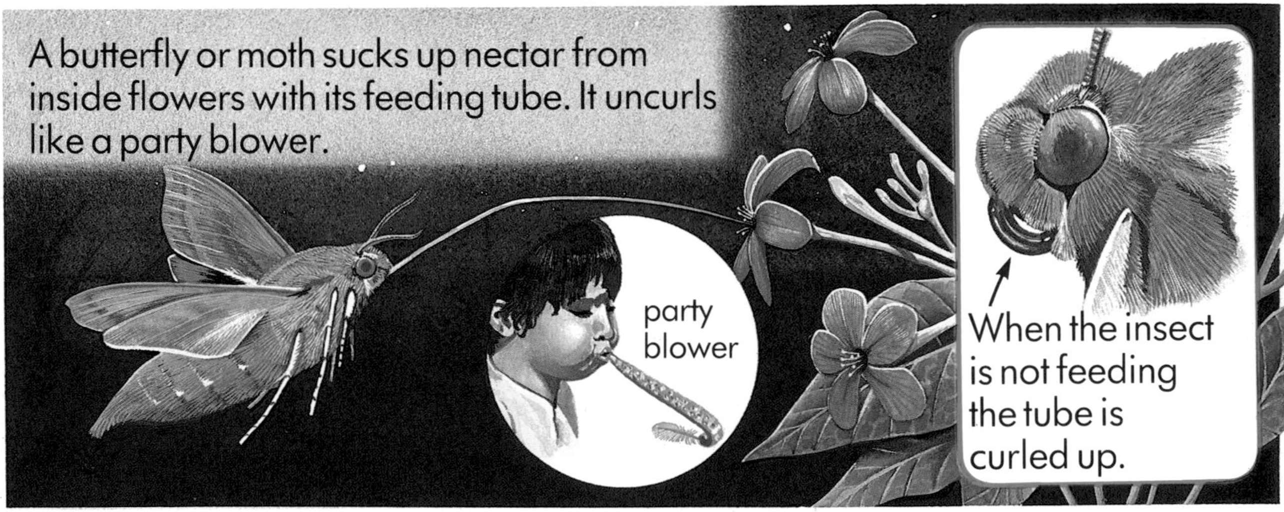

party
blower
When the insect
is not feeding
the tube is
curled up.

A butterfly or moth sucks up nectar from inside flowers with its feeding tube. It uncurls like a party blower.

A grasshopper's jaws work like a pair of pliers, nipping off bits of grass.

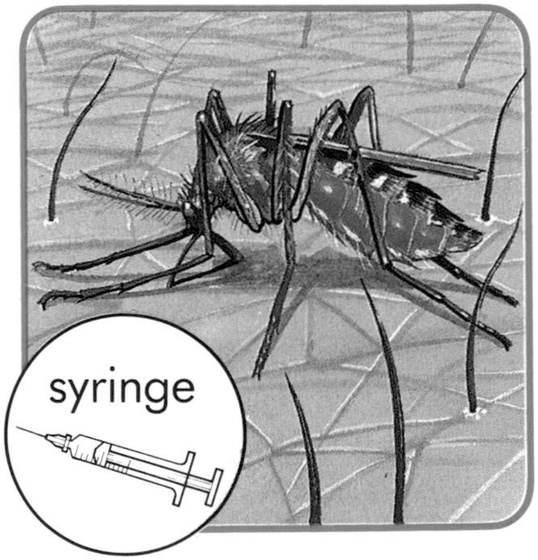

A female mosquito pierces the skin and sucks up blood, like a syringe.

The mouthparts of a fly soak up juices like a sponge mops up water.

Tarantula

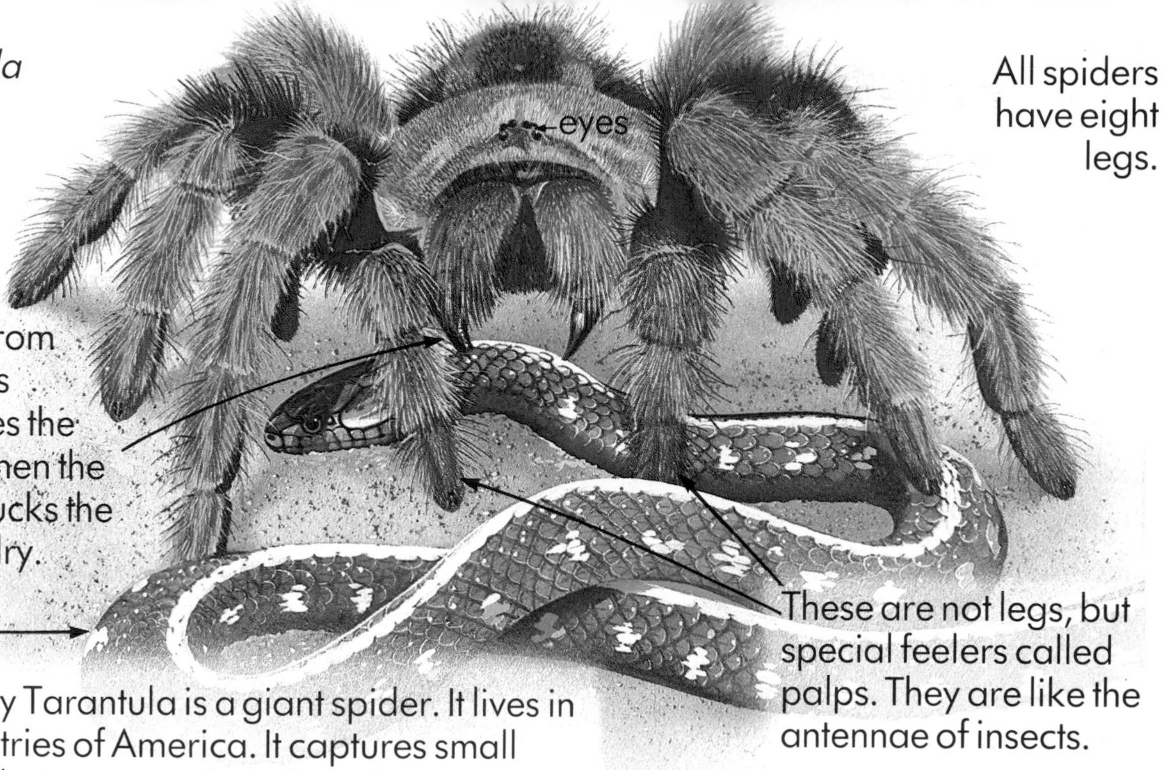

All spiders have eight legs.

Poison from the fangs paralyses the victim. Then the spider sucks the insides dry.

snake

These are not legs, but special feelers called palps. They are like the antennae of insects.

This hairy Tarantula is a giant spider. It lives in hot countries of America. It captures small mammals, insects and small snakes.

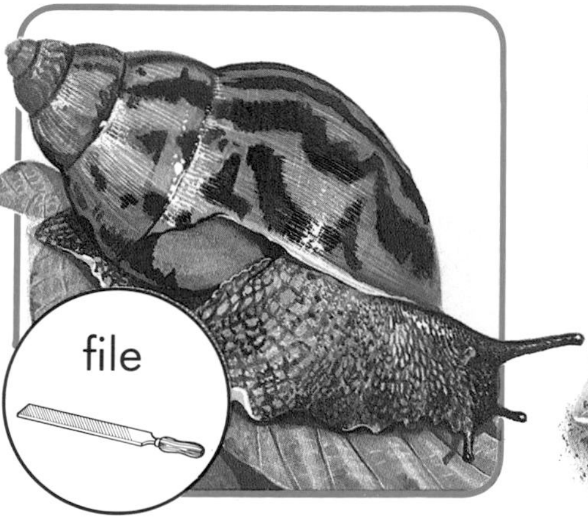

A snail's tongue is like a rough file. It feeds on leaves, fruit and flowers.

Burying Beetle

This beetle is digging soil from under the dead bird, so it is slowly buried.

Burying Beetles feed on dead animals they find. The females also lay their eggs on the body once it is buried. The young feed on the body when they hatch.

Colours and chemicals

Many invertebrates match the colour or the shape of their surroundings. They are camouflaged. If they keep still, they are difficult to see. Some invertebrates have bright colours to warn enemies not to touch. Others squirt harmful chemicals at their enemies.

The Peppered Moth is almost invisible on tree trunks.
The Thorn Bug looks like a thorn on a twig.
This Leaf Butterfly looks like a leaf when it is at rest.
This looper caterpillar looks like a twig.
big false eyes
abdomen
front legs

The Puss Moth caterpillar is camouflaged by its green body. It scares birds away by rearing its bright face and its tail.

The Flower Mantis looks like the flower on which it sits. Insects come to the flower to feed and get trapped by it.

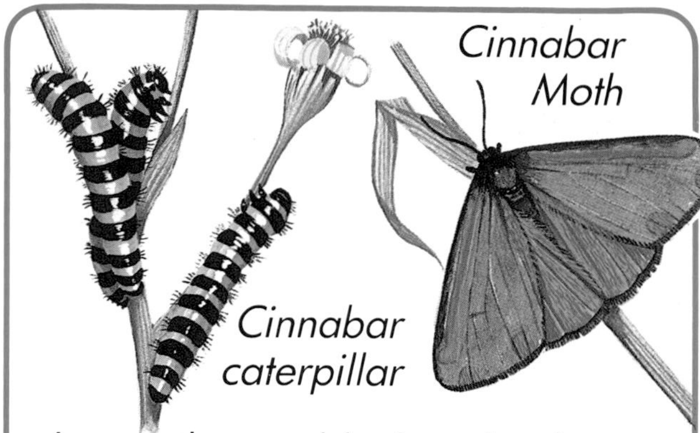

Insects that are black and red, or yellow or black, usually taste nasty. Birds learn to leave them alone.

This Wood Ant is ready for battle. In this position it can squirt acid at enemies that come too near.

If it is startled, the Bombardier Beetle fires a gas from its rear end that irritates the eyes of the enemy. The gas pops and also forms a smoke-screen. The beetle escapes while the enemy is confused. This drives off most enemies from ants, spiders and beetles to frogs and toads.

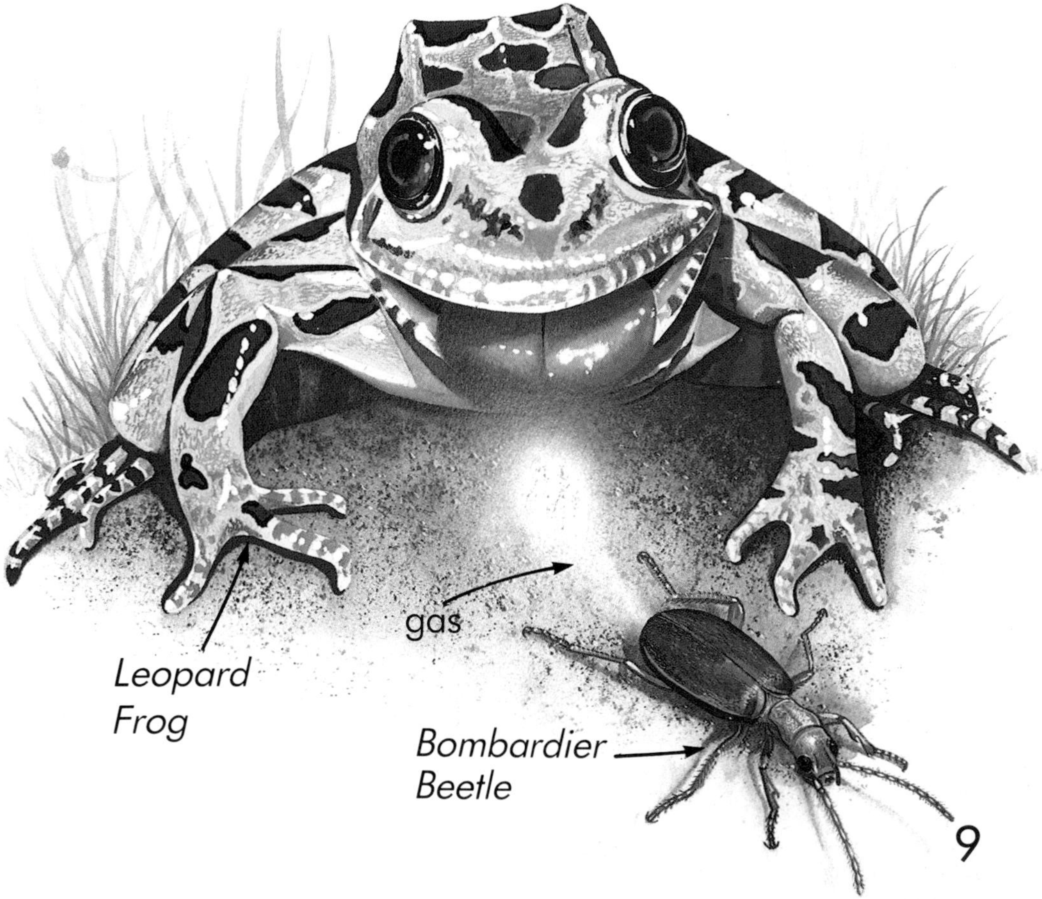

Eggs and young

Most female invertebrates lay eggs. These are usually quite small. The eggs are laid alone or in groups, in different places. Usually each egg is put where there is food for the young when it hatches. You may be able to find some eggs if you look at leaves or grasses.

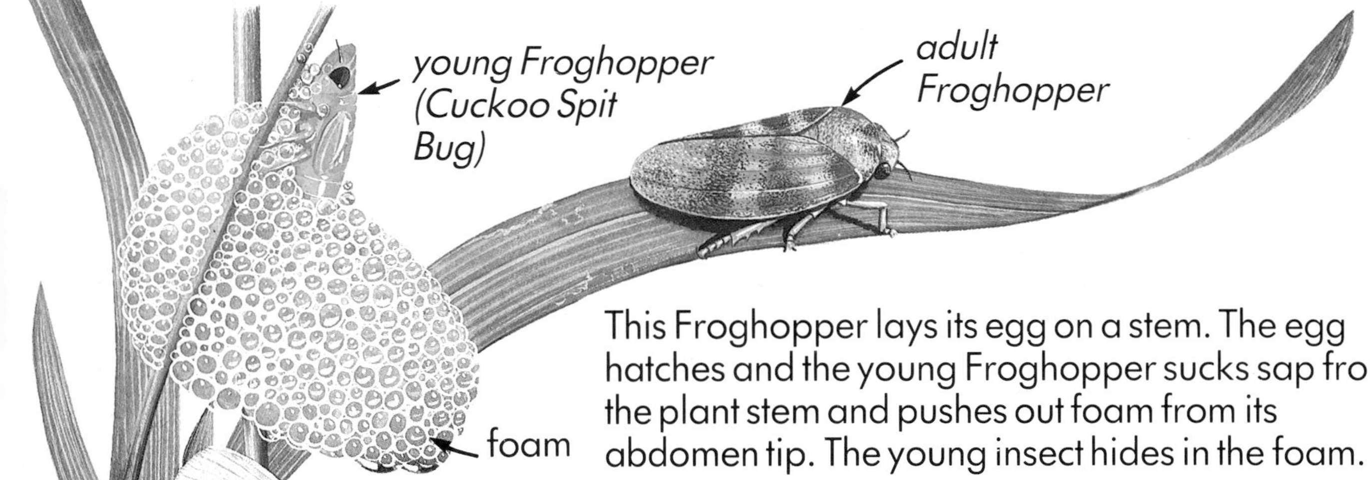

This Froghopper lays its egg on a stem. The egg hatches and the young Froghopper sucks sap from the plant stem and pushes out foam from its abdomen tip. The young insect hides in the foam.

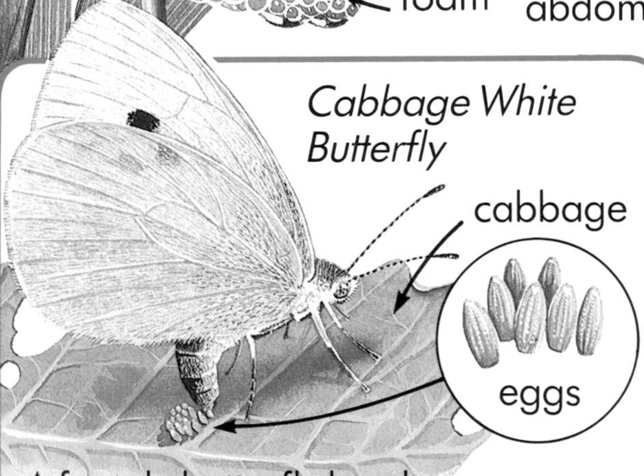

A female butterfly lays her eggs on a leaf. The caterpillars hatch and feed on it. She flies off and does not look after her eggs or young.

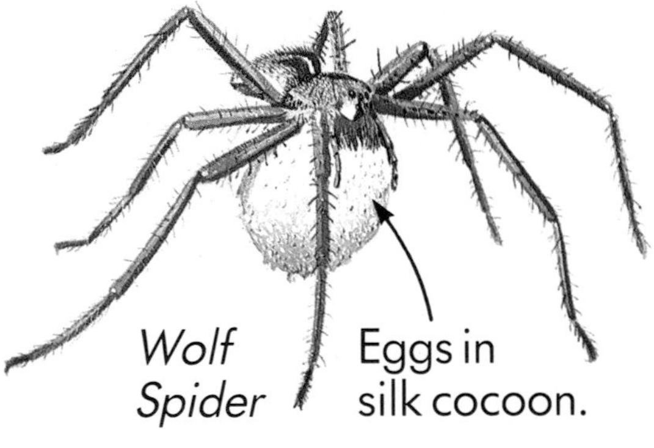

This female Wolf Spider spins a silk cocoon for her eggs. She carries it in her jaws until the eggs hatch.

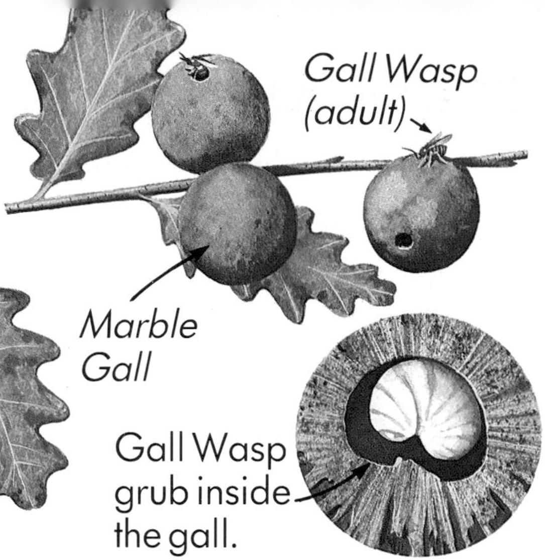

The Potter Wasp catches and paralyzes caterpillars. Then she pushes them into her clay pot. When it is full, she lays an egg inside. When the wasp grub hatches, it feeds on the caterpillars.

A Marble Gall is caused by a wasp that lays its egg in the bud of an oak. The oak swells around the grub and forms a gall. The wasp grub feeds on the gall until it changes into an adult wasp.

A snail lays lots of eggs in the soil, then leaves them to hatch by themselves. The young look like very tiny snails.

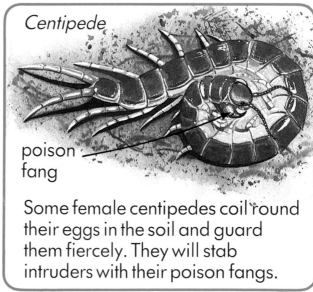

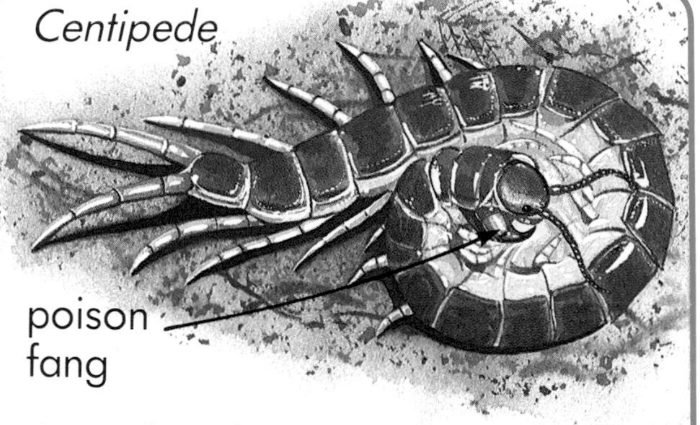

Some female centipedes coil round their eggs in the soil and guard them fiercely. They will stab intruders with their poison fangs.

Growing up

When a young invertebrate hatches, it often looks different from its parents. The young changes its appearance at least once before it becomes an adult. Some young invertebrates look like their parents when they are born or when they hatch.

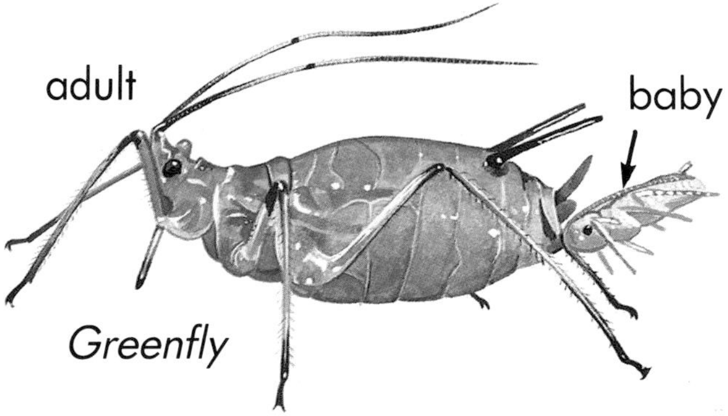

Some Greenfly do not lay eggs at all. They can give birth to babies without mating. The babies are tiny versions of the mother.

Female snails lay eggs. When the young hatch out, they look like very tiny adults. Their shells grow as the snails get bigger.

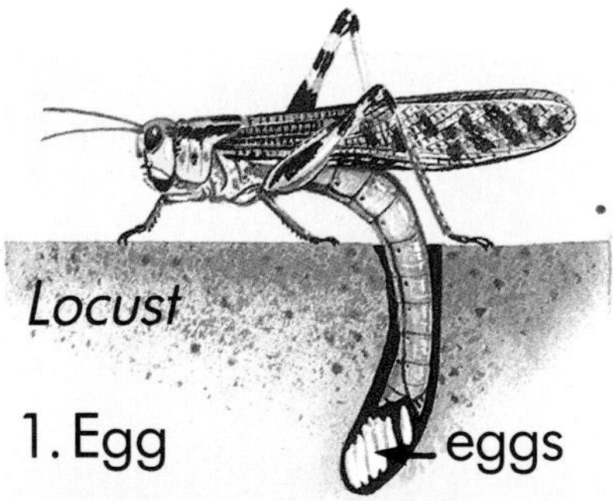

A female locust lays her eggs in damp, warm soil and leaves them to hatch.

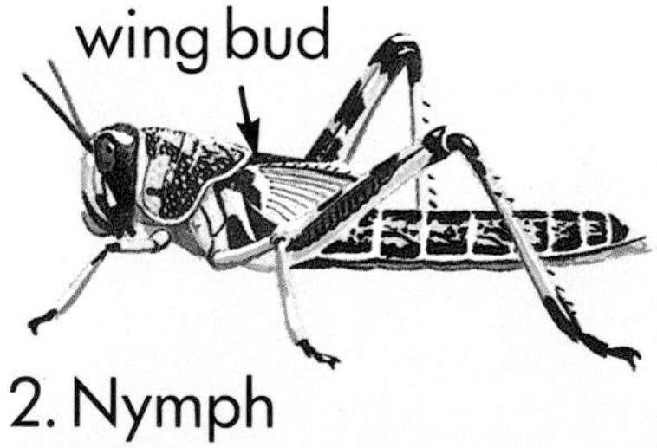

The young looks like an adult locust but has no wings, only wing buds.

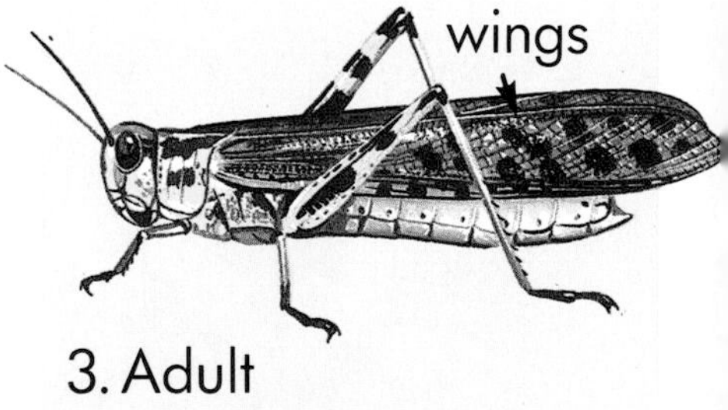

The nymph grows and changes into an adult. The adult has wings.

1. Eggs

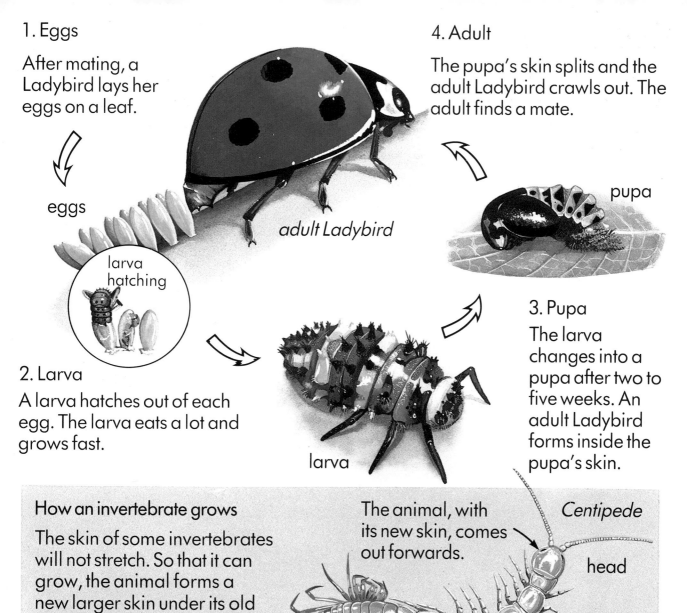

After mating, a Ladybird lays her eggs on a leaf.

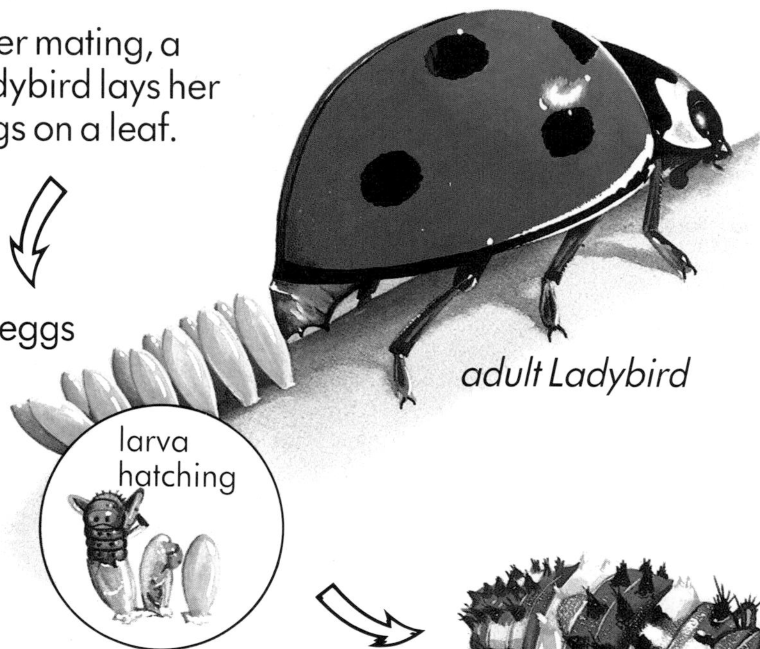

4. Adult

The pupa's skin splits and the adult Ladybird crawls out. The adult finds a mate.

2. Larva

A larva hatches out of each egg. The larva eats a lot and grows fast.

3. Pupa

The larva changes into a pupa after two to five weeks. An adult Ladybird forms inside the pupa's skin.

How an invertebrate grows

The skin of some invertebrates will not stretch. So that it can grow, the animal forms a new larger skin under its old skin. When this is ready, it splits open the old skin near the head and wriggles out.

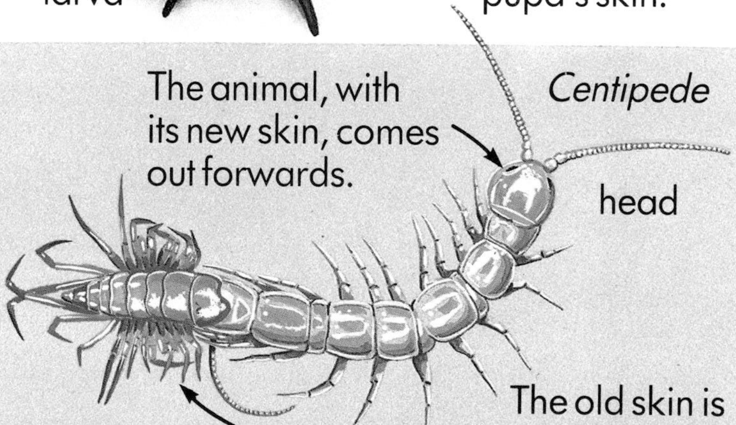

Spiders

Spiders live in many different places. Some live in our own homes and gardens. Others live on mountains or in deserts. Most of the 60,000 different kinds of spiders are very useful to us. They eat lots of flies and other pests. All spiders have eight legs and can spin silk.

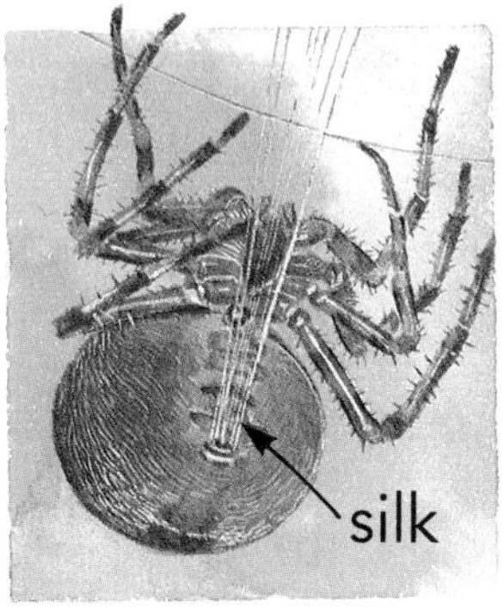

Silk is made by special organs in the abdomen.

This spider spins a silk thread as an escape line.

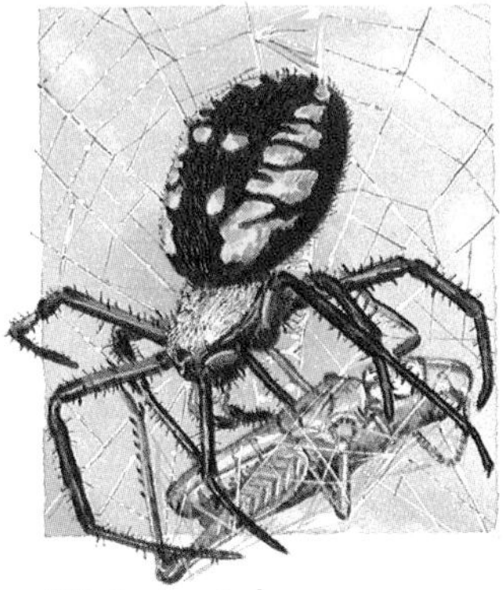

This spider wraps its prey in silken threads.

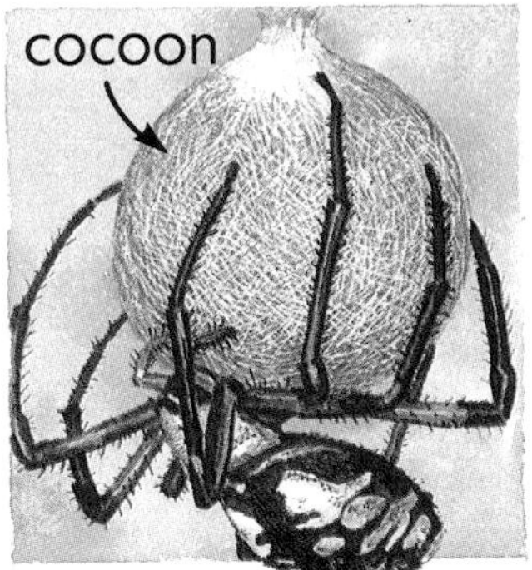

Spiders spin a silk cocoon to protect their eggs.

An Orb Spider waits for its prey to become trapped in its web. The spider does not get stuck on its own web because it has oil on its feet.

This tiny Crab Spider looks like the flower it sits on. It waits in ambush for passing insects such as bees, then grabs one in its fangs.

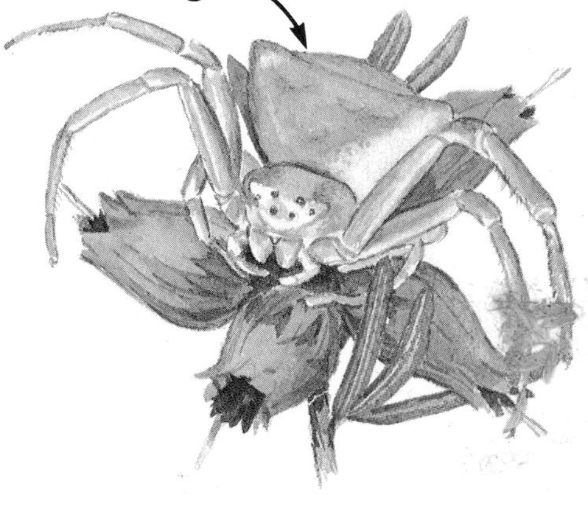

The deadly ones

All spiders have sharp fangs with poison to paralyze or kill their prey. A few spiders are dangerous and can hurt people. Here are three of them.

In the United States, the female's poison is stronger than elsewhere. It can kill people.

The Red Back of Australia is called the Night Stinger in New Zealand.

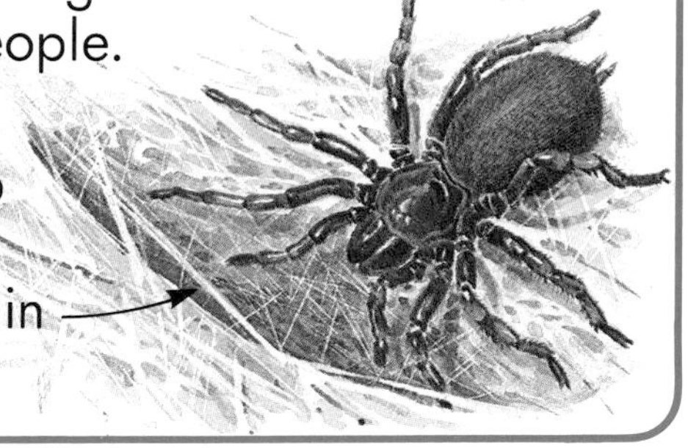

This Funnelweb Spider lives around Sydney in Australia.

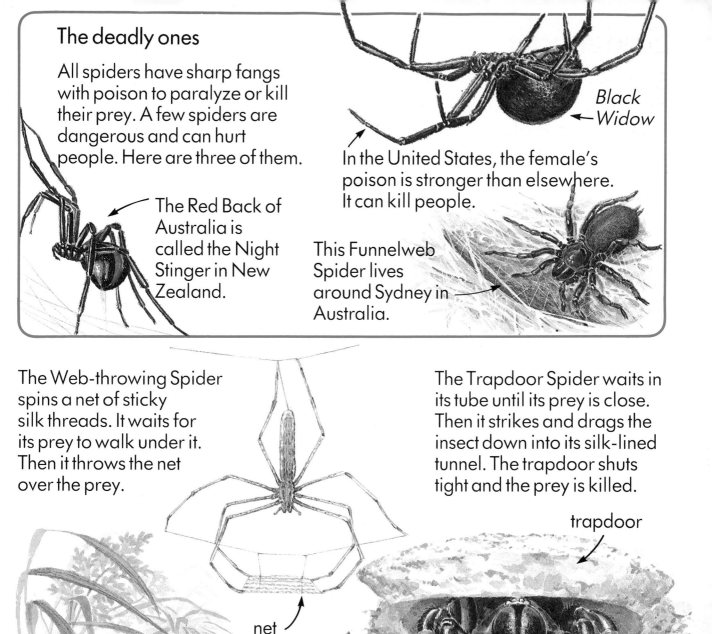

The Web-throwing Spider spins a net of sticky silk threads. It waits for its prey to walk under it. Then it throws the net over the prey.

The Trapdoor Spider waits in its tube until its prey is close. Then it strikes and drags the insect down into its silk-lined tunnel. The trapdoor shuts tight and the prey is killed.

Slugs and snails

Slugs and snails belong to the group called gastropods. This means "bellyfoots". Slugs are land snails that have no shell.

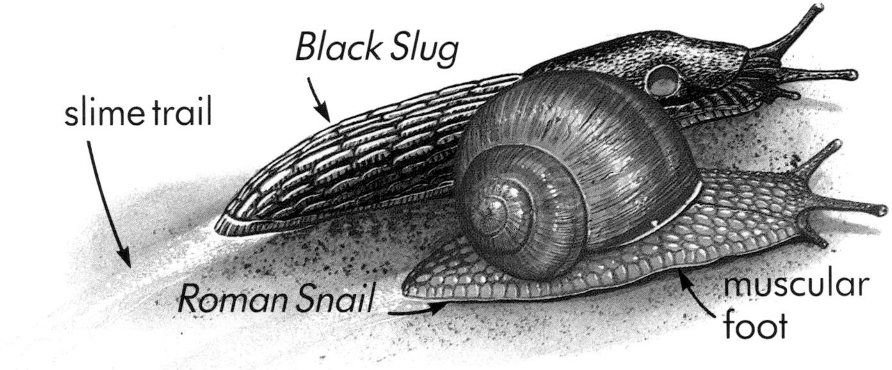

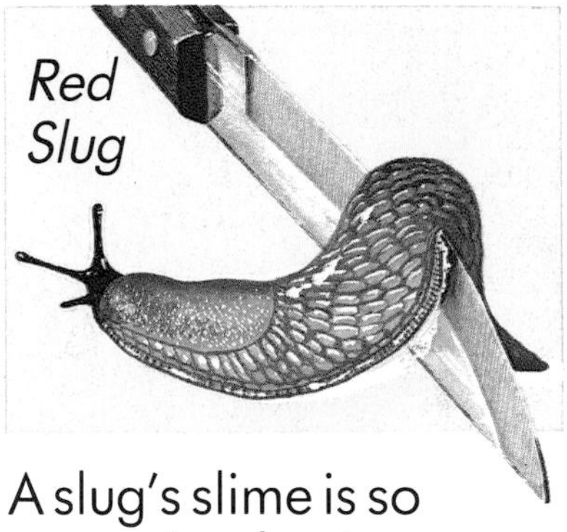

Slugs and snails make a slimy substance that helps them move along. They leave a slime trail. The flat underpart of their body is called a muscular foot.

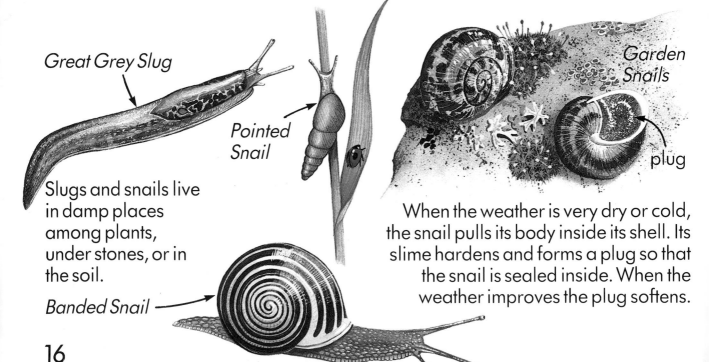

A slug's slime is so protective that it can climb over a very sharp knife unharmed.

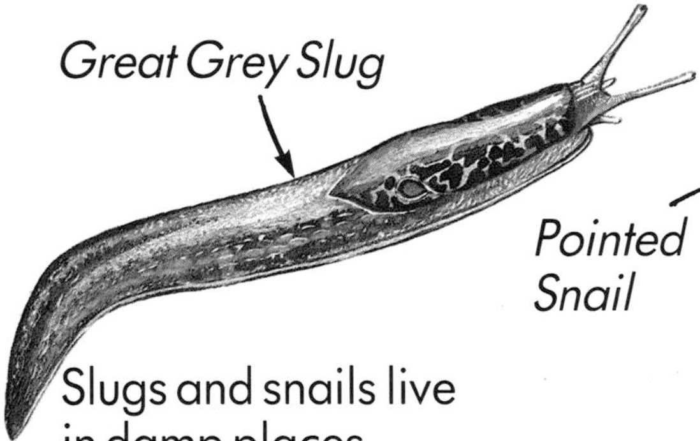

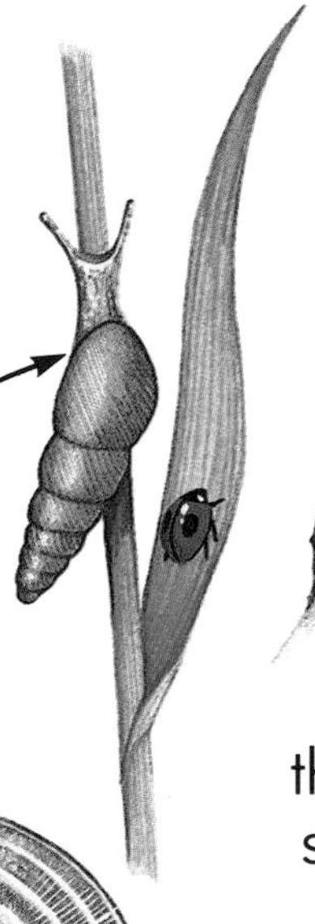

Slugs and snails live in damp places among plants, under stones, or in the soil.

When the weather is very dry or cold, the snail pulls its body inside its shell. Its slime hardens and forms a plug so that the snail is sealed inside. When the weather improves the plug softens.

There are Giant Snails in many parts of the world. This one comes from West Africa. One of the largest snails ever found measured 34 centimetres from the top of its shell to the tip of its head. Giant Snails eat all kinds of plants and their fruits, including bananas. They also eat dead animals.

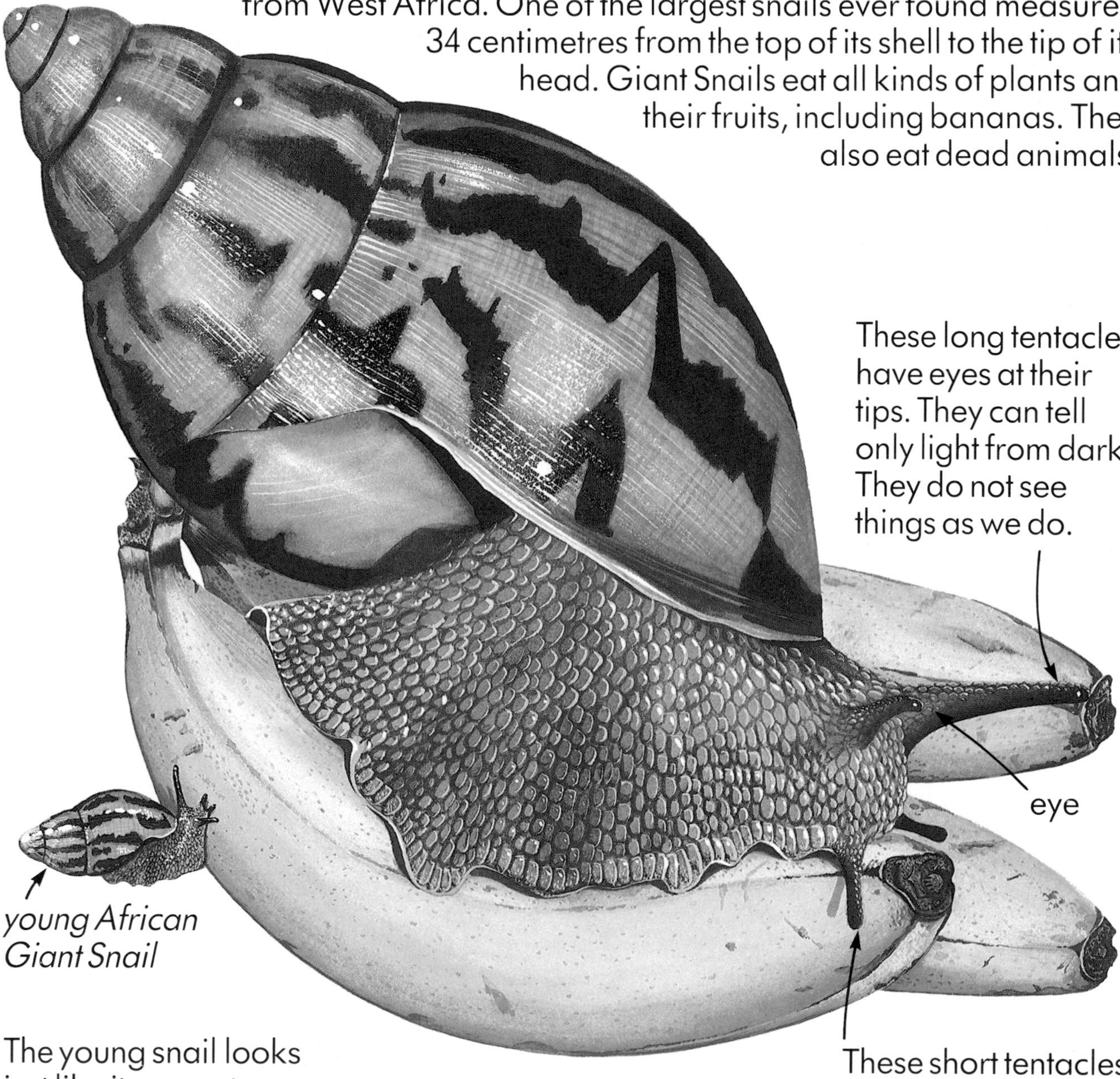

These long tentacles have eyes at their tips. They can tell only light from dark. They do not see things as we do.

These short tentacles smell and feel things. They have no eyes.

The young snail looks just like its parent.

Beetles

There are over 250,000 different kinds of beetles. Turn over a log in a forest or disturb some fallen leaves. You are likely to find a beetle.

Most beetles are quite small. A few grow to the size of these two beetles. They are drawn life size.

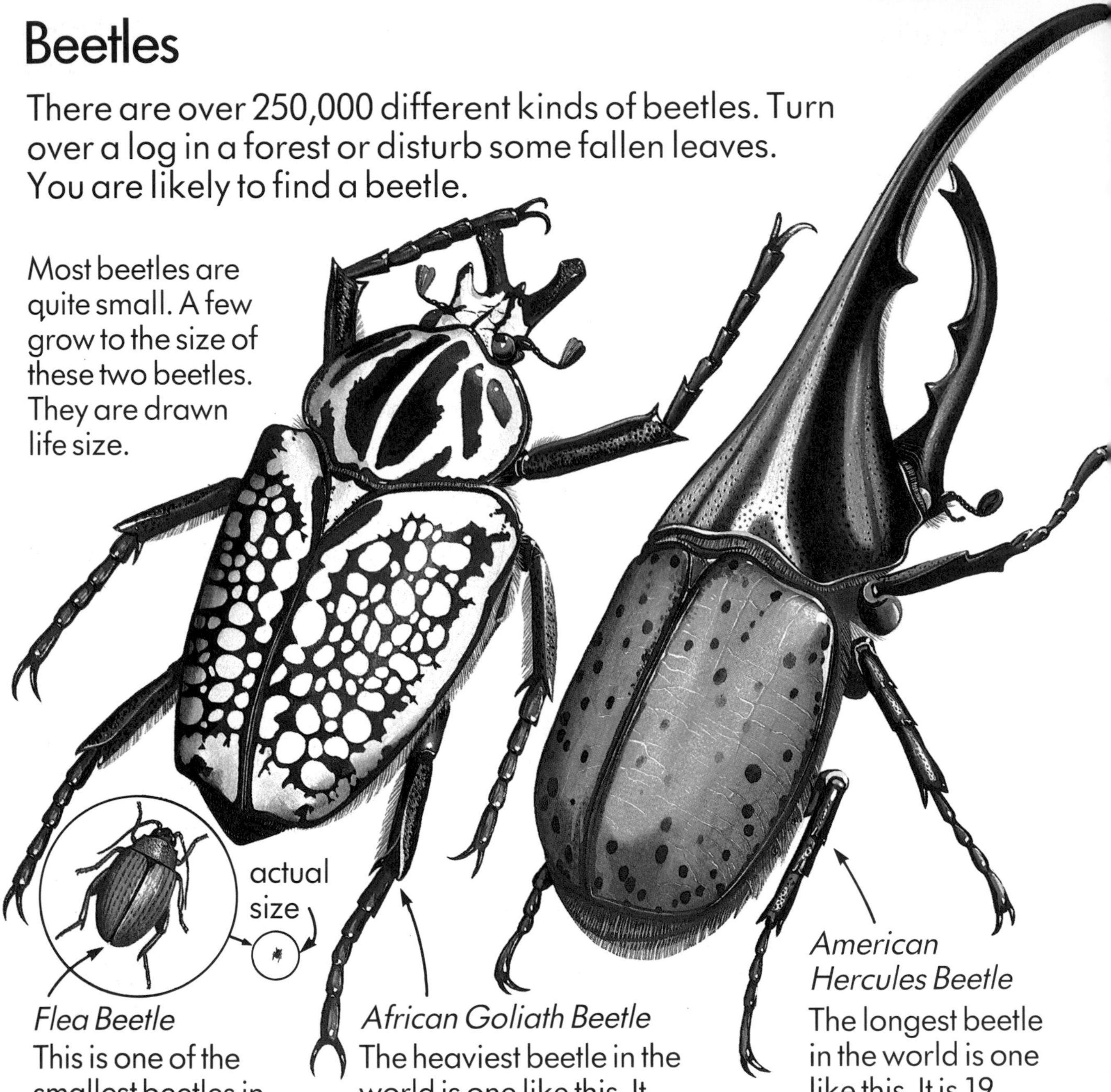

Flea Beetle
This is one of the smallest beetles in the world.

African Goliath Beetle
The heaviest beetle in the world is one like this. It weighs 100 grams.

American Hercules Beetle
The longest beetle in the world is one like this. It is 19 centimetres long.

Helpful beetles

This beetle was brought into America from its home in Australia. It eats the scale insect pests that damage orange and lemon trees in California.

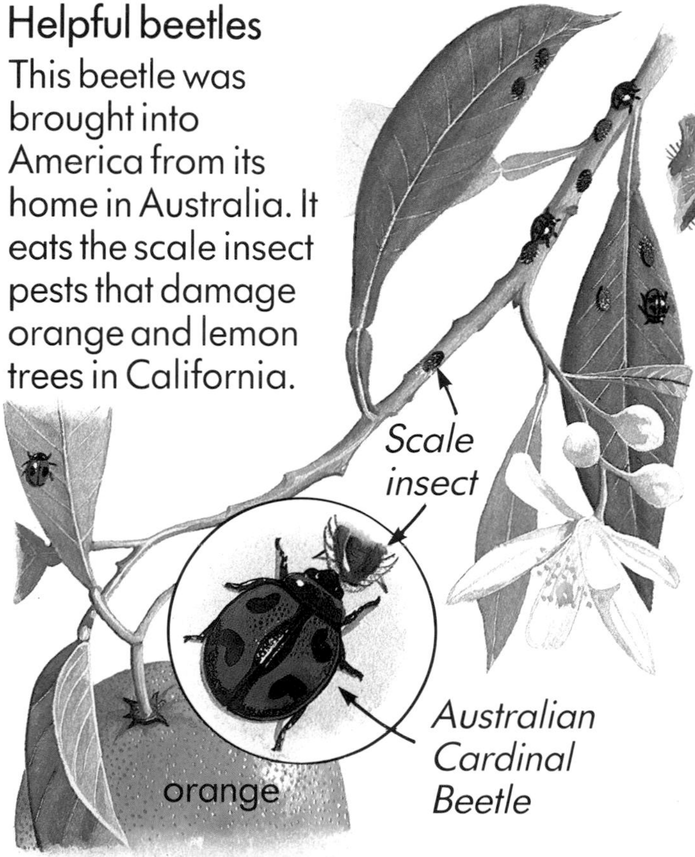

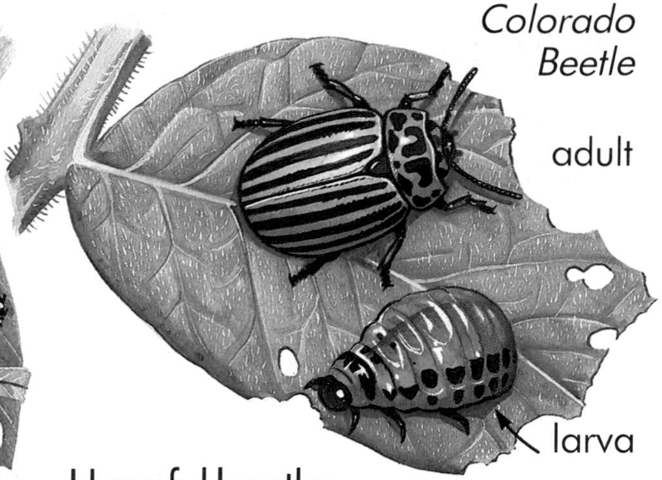

Harmful beetles

Colorado Beetles and their larvae eat the leaves of potato plants. Their home is in the United States but they have travelled to most places where potatoes are grown. They can destroy a whole potato crop.

Living lanterns

Fireflies and Glow-worms are not flies or worms. They are beetles. Both insects can produce light at the tip of their bodies. They use light to attract a mate. In hot countries you can see trees lit up by fireflies flashing.

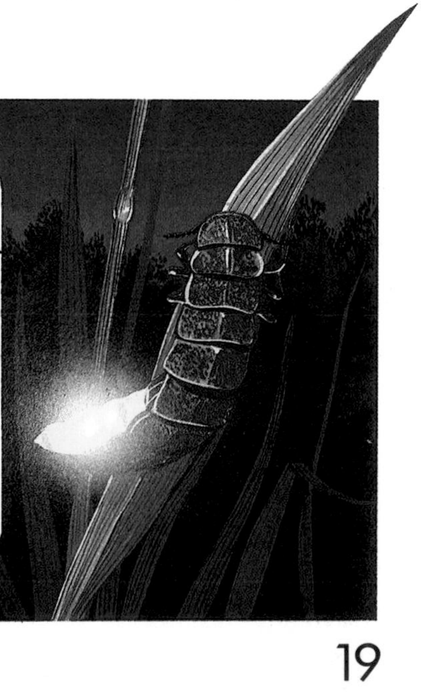

Termite cities

Some insects live and work together in large family groups. They are called social insects. Termites, ants, and some bees and wasps are social insects. Some termites build huge mounds or nests. Most termites live in hot countries and feed on wood.

Jungle termite nests

A new roof is added each year.

Termite nest cut in half to show passages inside.

In tropical rain forests, where it rains a lot, termites build their nests with a roof. This works like an umbrella. It keeps heavy rain from damaging the nest.

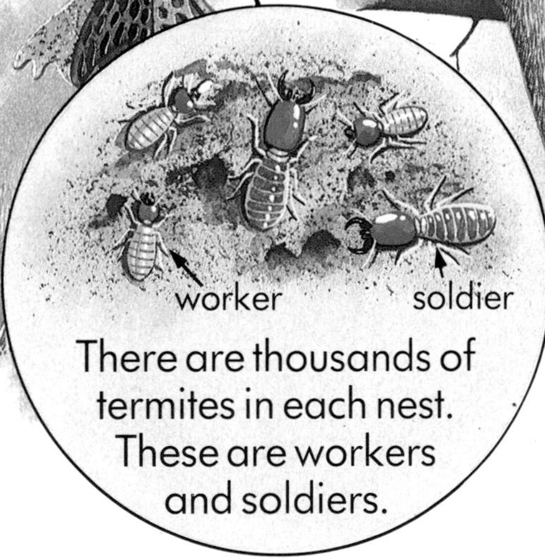

There are thousands of termites in each nest. These are workers and soldiers.

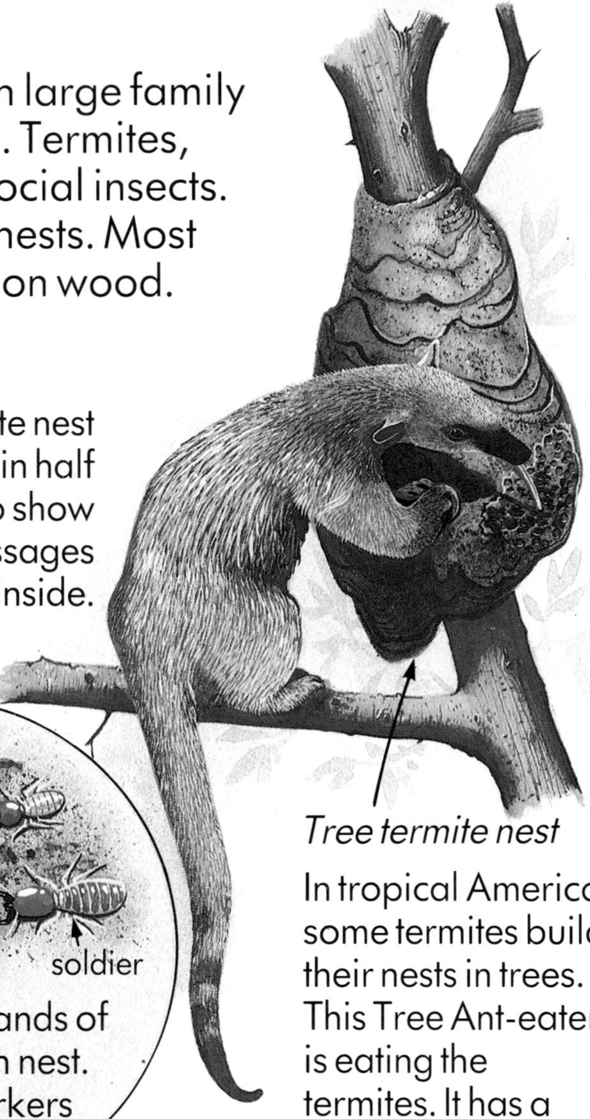

Tree termite nest

In tropical America some termites build their nests in trees. This Tree Ant-eater is eating the termites. It has a long, sticky tongue.

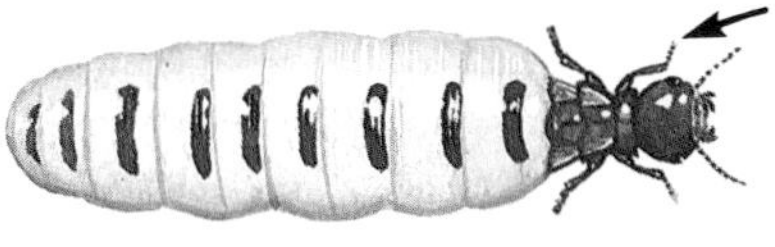

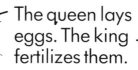

The queen lays eggs. The king fertilizes them.

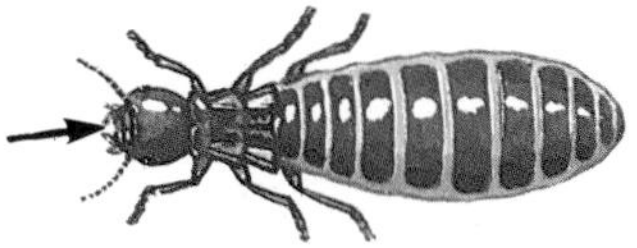

Some African termite nests are built higher than a giraffe. A record one reached 12.8 metres in height. This is over twice the height of a giraffe.

In northern Australia the Compass Termites build nests with flattened sides. They have two narrow sides and two broad sides. The broad sides always face east and west. They catch the sun's rays at sunrise and sunset, when the rays are not too strong. At mid-day the rays are strong, but shine on the narrow sides, so the termites do not get too hot.

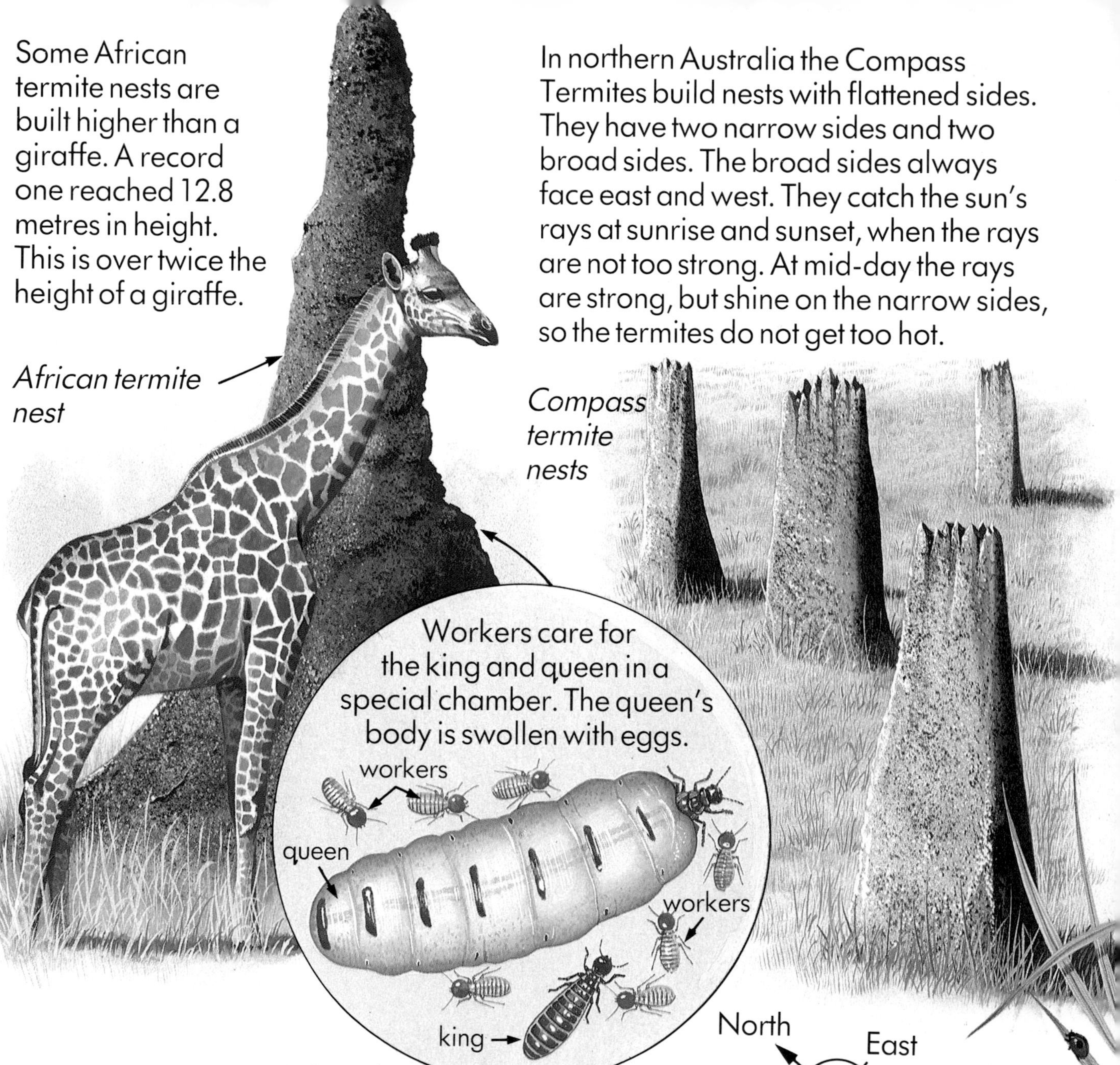

Workers care for the king and queen in a special chamber. The queen's body is swollen with eggs.

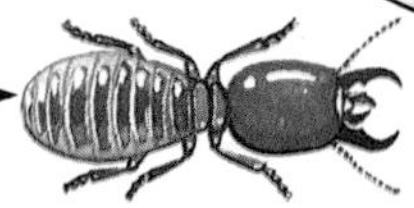
Soldier termites guard the nest.

Amazing creepy crawlies

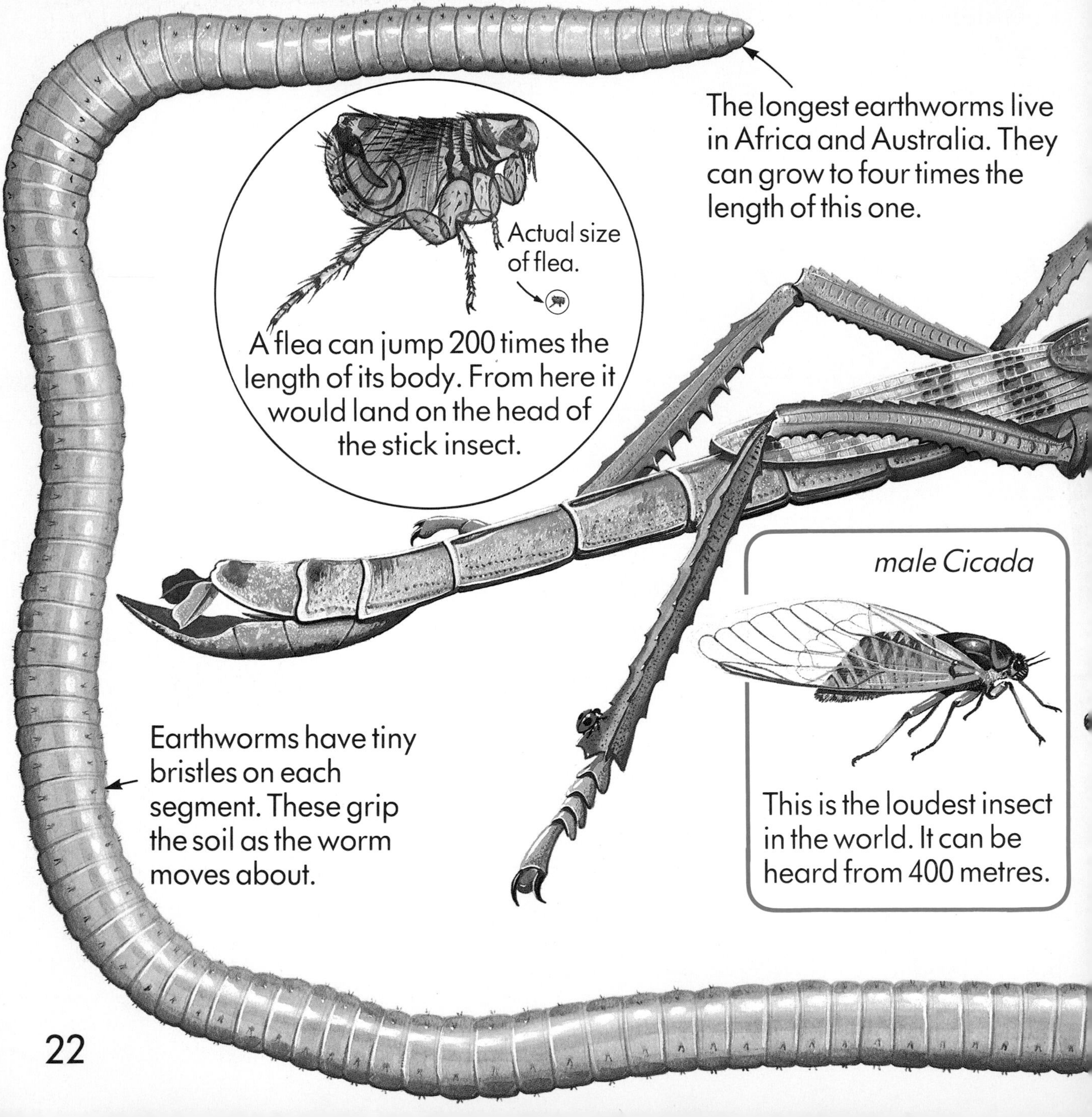

The longest earthworms live in Africa and Australia. They can grow to four times the length of this one.

Actual size of flea.

A flea can jump 200 times the length of its body. From here it would land on the head of the stick insect.

male Cicada

This is the loudest insect in the world. It can be heard from 400 metres.

Earthworms have tiny bristles on each segment. These grip the soil as the worm moves about.

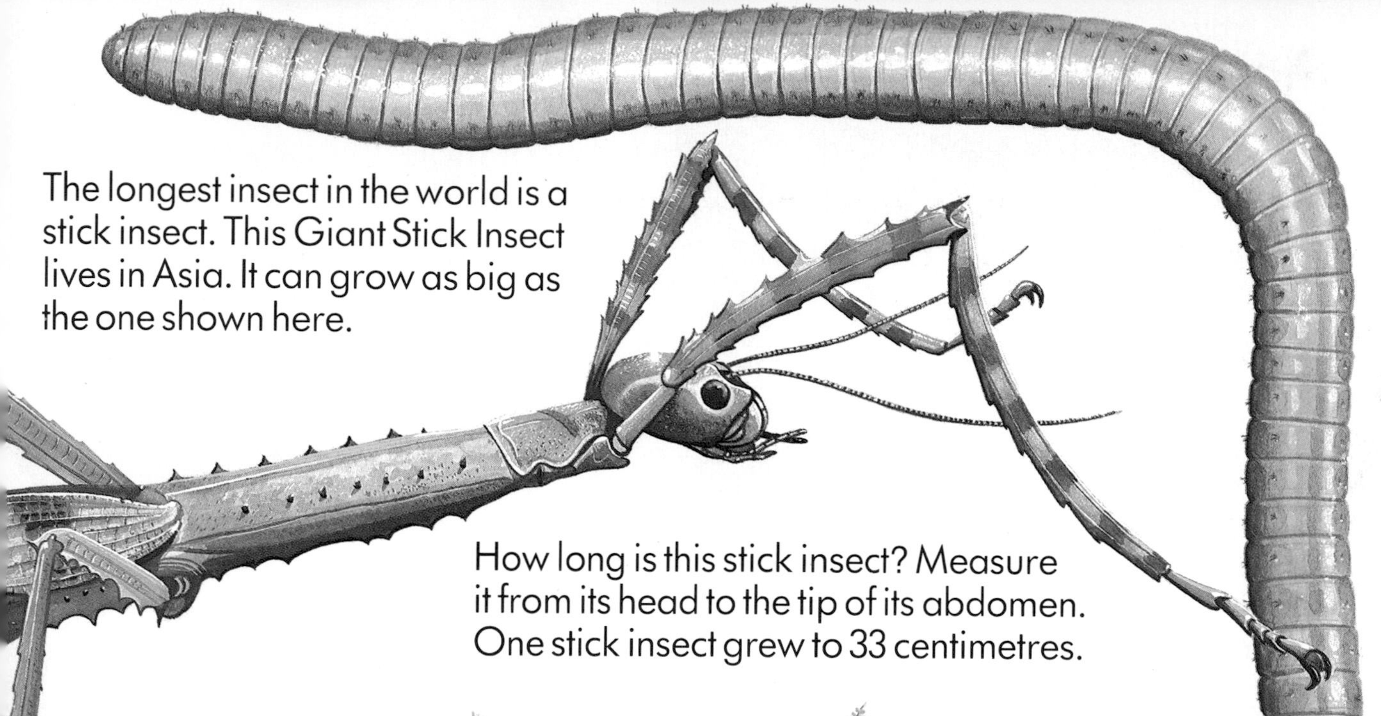

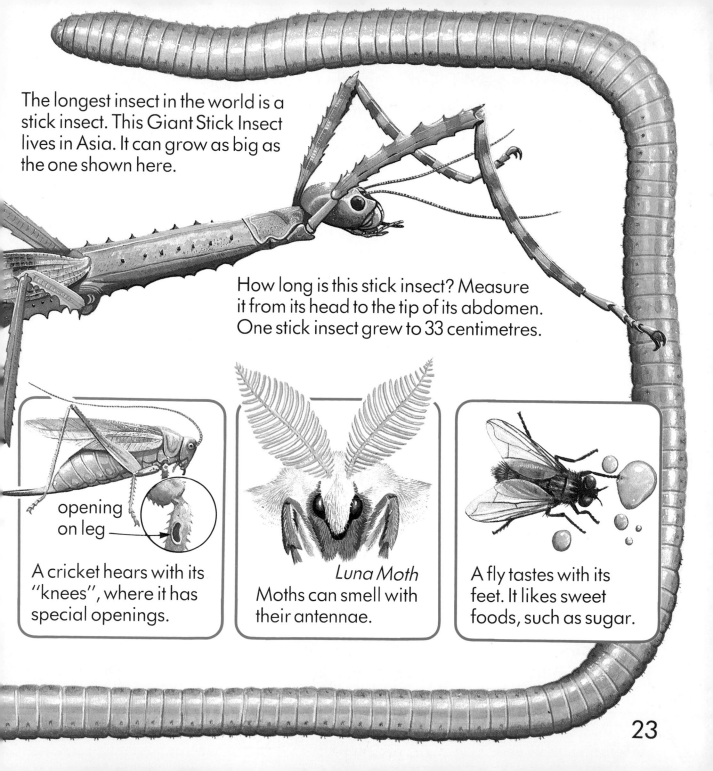

The longest insect in the world is a stick insect. This Giant Stick Insect lives in Asia. It can grow as big as the one shown here.

How long is this stick insect? Measure it from its head to the tip of its abdomen. One stick insect grew to 33 centimetres.

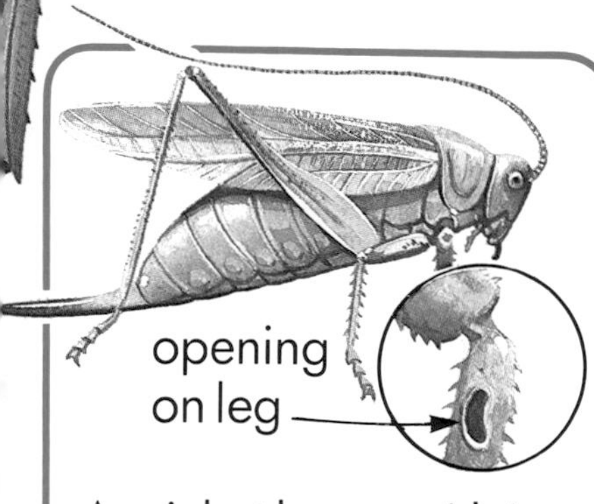

A cricket hears with its "knees", where it has special openings.

Luna Moth

Moths can smell with their antennae.

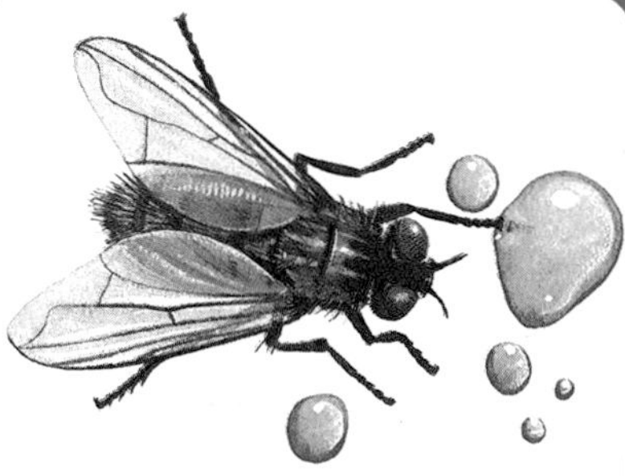

A fly tastes with its feet. It likes sweet foods, such as sugar.

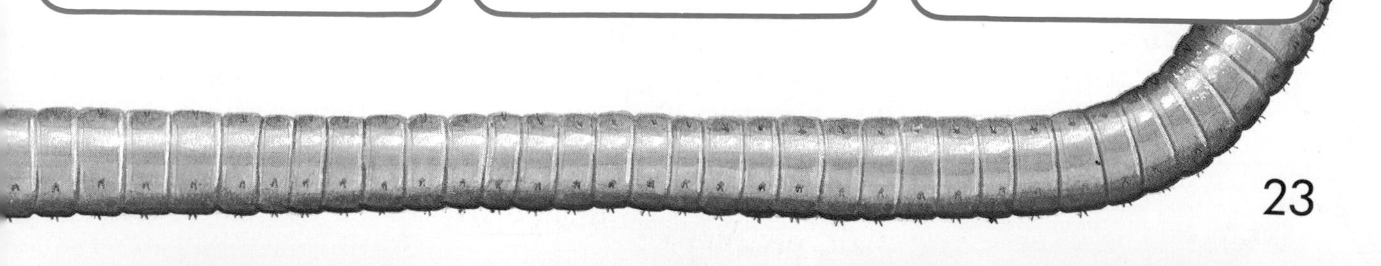

Picture puzzle

All the invertebrates shown below have one or more things wrong with their bodies. Can you see what is wrong with each one? You can find them all in this book. The answers are at the bottom of the page.

Answers: 1, Fly should have only one pair of large wings. 2, Grasshopper's back legs should be larger. 3, Caterpillar shouldn't have legs on each segment. 4, Spider should have 8 legs. 5, Scorpion's sting and pincers are in wrong positions. 6, Ladybird should have 6 legs. 7, Beetle shouldn't have feathery antennae. 8, Snail should have two pairs of tentacles and its mouth and eyes are in the wrong place. 9, Earthworm should have no legs, no eyes and no tongue.

First published in 1982. Usborne Publishing Ltd, Usborne House, 83-85 Saffron Hill, London EC1N 8RT. Printed in Belgium. UE